Fun Treats

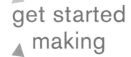

get started
making

Fun
Treats

step-by-step recipes
for everyday surprises

Little Miss Bento
Shirley Wong

Marshall Cavendish
Cuisine

Shirley Wong, better known by her online avatar Little Miss Bento, became an online sensation and gained a huge following when she started posting her cute food creations and recipes on her blog and social media channels.

Currently the top bento artist, food stylist and blogger based in Singapore, Shirley has won many awards for her foodart creations and has been featured in numerous local and international media platforms and publications.

A huge fan of the kawaii culture and a strong believer that home-style food should be simple and achievable, Shirley shares easy recipes for cute sweets and snacks in this brand new cookbook.

Find out more about Shirley and her creations on her blog and social media channels.

Blog | littlemissbento.com
Facebook | www.facebook.com/littlemissbento
Instagram | Twitter | Snapchat | Pinterest | @littlemissbento
Email | littlemissbento@gmail.com

I would like to dedicate this book to my father, whom I believe I 'inherited' my sweet tooth from. His constant support has motivated me to continue to pursue my passion and love for cooking.

Contents

Introduction

Many cultures around the world incorporate a midday break, a time out or interlude in the middle of everyday demands to relax, socialise and enjoy a beverage with baked goods. In this book I have tried to make this daily ritual easy, fun and hopefully put a smile on people's faces.

From doughnuts shaped as bears, bees and watermelons to bao formed as pandas, chicks, mushrooms and roses to teddy bear wagashi, the kawaii treats shared in this cookbook will appeal to those with a sweet tooth, or those who would like a petite surprise with their daily coffee or tea. The confections are also perfect for offering a guest or tucked into a child's snack box.

So go on, take a break and make tea time something to look forward to.

Little Miss Bento
Shirley Wong

Rolling Home-made Piping Bags

In general for making cute baking goods, I find that it is often necessary to pipe small designs. Home-made piping bags give the user more control and are suitable for piping small portions of batter as compared to regular plastic piping bags. A second advantage is that piping heads and tips are not needed with home-made piping bags. To start, trim the parchment paper into a triangle. On the flat end, roll the parchment paper into a small tight cone. Staple the ends to keep them together.

Basic Bao Dough

~~~ Ingredients ~~~

Bao flour/Hong Kong flour
  85 g + more as needed

Sugar 10 g

Instant dry yeast 2 g

Warm milk or soymilk 45 ml
  (no more than 40°C, or
  the yeast will get killed)

Salad oil $^1/_2$ Tbsp

Salt $^1/_3$ tsp

**Purple sweet potato
  powder** 1 tsp (for
  colouring, optional)

Matcha powder $^1/_4$ tsp (for
  colouring, optional)

1. Sift and divide flour into two portions.

2. Combine one portion of flour with sugar and dry yeast in a mixing bowl.

3. Add milk or soymilk. Mix well with a wooden spatula.

4. Add salad oil and salt. Add remaining portion of flour and mix well into a dough. Dough should not be smooth yet. Scrape and transfer from bowl to floured surface.

5. Knead for a few minutes until dough is even. The dough should be smooth and soft, and not stick to your hands. Shape dough into a ball.

6. To colour the dough, portion out as required and add desired colouring.

7. Cover with cling wrap and allow dough to rest for about 30 minutes for fermentation to take place. The size of the dough should increase about 1.5 times.

8. Punch dough down gently 3–4 times to remove air.

9. Divide and shape the dough as desired.

10. Place bao on parchment paper and steam for about 15 minutes. Steaming time required may differ depending on the size of bao and the choice of fillings.

Bumblebee Doughnuts

Makes 6 doughnuts

~~~~~~~~~~~~~~~~~~~~ Ingredients ~~~~~~~~~~~~~~~~~~~~

Milk 100 ml

Whipping cream 75 g

Melted butter 1 Tbsp + more for greasing

Egg 1, medium

Honey 2 Tbsp

Vanilla essence 5 drops

Morinaga hot cake mix 150 g

Cake flour 1 tsp

Black cocoa powder or varlhona dark cocoa powder 1 tsp

Yellow icing colour a few drops

TOOLS

Silicon doughnut moulds

Home-made piping bags (page 12)

Parchment paper

Small sharp knife

Method

1. Preheat oven to 180°C. Grease doughnut moulds. Set aside.

2. Combine milk, whipping cream, butter, egg, honey and vanilla essence in a large bowl. Mix well using a hand whisk.

3. Add hot cake mix in 2–3 parts, mixing well with each addition to ensure that there are no lumps.

4. Add 4 tsp batter to cake flour in a small bowl. Mix well. Spoon batter into a piping bag.

5. Add 4 tsp batter to black cocoa powder in a clean separate bowl. Mix well. Spoon batter into a piping bag.

6. Add yellow icing colour to remaining batter. Mix well.

7. Using the piping bag containing black cocoa powder batter, pipe outlines for the bee onto prepared mould.

8. Place in oven. Bake for 1.5 minutes.

9. Remove mould from oven. Spoon yellow batter evenly into doughnut moulds until 90% full. Level surface with a teaspoon.

10. Bake for 14–15 minutes.

11. Pipe design for the wings and feelers onto parchment paper. Bake for 2–3 minutes.

12. Using a skewer and small sharp knife, make small holes and slits for each doughnut. Place feelers and wings into the slits to complete the bumblebee character.

Note

Allow doughnuts to cool down on a wire rack before removing from the moulds to prevent the designs from falling apart.

Cute Bear Doughnuts

Makes 6 doughnuts

~~~~~~~~~~~~ Ingredients ~~~~~~~~~~~~

Milk 100 ml

Whipping cream 75 g

Honey 2 Tbsp

Egg 1, medium

Melted butter 1 Tbsp + more for greasing

Vanilla essence 5 drops

Morinaga hot cake mix 150 g

Cake flour $^1/_2$ tsp

Black cocoa powder or varlhona dark cocoa powder $^1/_2$ tsp

Earl grey powder or houjicha powder 2 tsp

TOOLS

Silicon doughnut moulds

Home-made piping bags (page 12)

Parchment paper

Small sharp knife

1. Preheat oven to 180°C. Grease doughnut moulds. Set aside.

2. Combine milk, whipping cream, egg, honey, butter and vanilla essence in a large bowl. Mix well using a whisk.

3. Add hot cake mix in 2–3 parts, mixing well with each addition to ensure that there are no lumps.

4. Add 2 tsp batter to cake flour in a small bowl. Mix well. Spoon batter into a piping bag.

5. Add 2 tsp batter to black cocoa powder in a separate bowl. Mix well. Spoon batter into a piping bag.

6. Sift earl grey powder into remaining hot cake batter in a clean separate bowl. Mix well.

7. Using the piping bag containing black cocoa powder batter, pipe eyes and nose of the bear into doughnut mould.

8. Bake for 1 minute.

9. Remove mould from oven. Pour earl grey batter evenly into doughnut moulds until 90% full. Level surface with a teaspoon.

10. Bake for 14–15 minutes.

11. Pipe ears of bear onto parchment paper. Bake for 2 minutes.

12. Using a small sharp knife, make slits for each doughnut. Place ears into the slits to complete the bear character.

Note

Allow doughnuts to cool down on a wire rack before removing from the moulds to prevent the designs from falling apart.

Watermelon Doughnuts

Makes 6 doughnuts

~~~~~ Ingredients ~~~~~

Milk 100 ml

Whipping cream 75 g

Melted butter 1 Tbsp +
more for greasing

Egg 1, medium

Honey 2 Tbsp

Vanilla essence 5 drops

Morinaga hot cake mix
150 g

Pink or red food colour
a few drops

Cake flour 1 tsp

**Black cocoa powder or
varlhona dark cocoa
powder** 1/2 tsp

Matcha powder 4 g

TOOLS

Silicon doughnut mould

**Home-made piping bags
(page 12)**

Method

1. Preheat oven to 180°C. Grease doughnut moulds. Set aside.

2. Combine milk, whipping cream, butter, egg, honey and vanilla essence in large bowl. Mix well with a hand whisk.

3. Add hot cake mix in 2–3 parts, mixing well with each addition to ensure that there are no lumps.

4. Add 4 tsp batter to pink or red food colouring and cake flour in a small bowl. Mix well. Spoon batter into a piping bag.

5. Add 4 tsp batter to black cocoa powder in a separate clean bowl. Mix well. Spoon batter into a piping bag.

6. Add matcha powder to remaining batter. Mix well.

7. Using the piping bag containing black cocoa powder batter, pipe small dots to form the watermelon seeds.

8. Place in oven. Bake for 1 minute.

9. Remove mould from oven.

10. Using the piping bag containing pink or red batter, pipe several rounds for the flesh of the watermelon.

11. Place in oven. Bake for 1 minute.

12. Remove mould from oven.

13. Spoon matcha batter evenly into doughnut moulds until 90% full. Level surface with a teaspoon.

14. Bake for 14–15 minutes.

Note

Allow doughnuts to cool down on a wire rack before removing from the moulds to prevent the designs from falling apart.

Matcha Twists

Makes 15 matcha twists

~~~~~~ Ingredients ~~~~~~

Milk 20 ml

Matcha powder 1 $^1/_2$ tsp, sifted

Condensed milk 3 Tbsp

Plain (all-purpose) flour 80 g

Puff pastry 2 sheets

Egg yolk 1

Water a few drops

TOOLS

Pastry brush

1. Preheat oven to 180°C. Line a baking tray with parchment paper. Set aside.

2. Place milk in a heatproof bowl. Warm milk in microwave.

3. Add matcha powder and mix well.

4. Add condensed milk and flour. Mix well to remove any lumps.

5. Spread a thin layer of matcha mixture on one sheet of frozen puff pastry.

6. Top with another sheet of puff pastry.

7. Lightly whisk the egg yolk with a few drops of water to make an egg wash. Using a pastry brush, brush egg wash on the puff pastry.

8. Cut into 15 thin long strips of 2 x 30-cm lengths.

9. Twist them and place on prepared baking tray.

10. Bake for 15–18 minutes.

Teddy Momoyama Wagashi

Makes 6 wagashi

~~~~~~~~ Ingredients ~~~~~~~~

Egg yolk ¹/₂

Mirin 1 tsp

***FOR MOMOYAMA
WAGASHI***

**White bean paste
(*shiro-an*)** 100 g

Egg yolk 1

**Cooked rice flour (*kanpai*
powder)** 1 Tbsp

Mirin 1 tsp

FOR MATCHA AN PASTE

Matcha powder 8 g, sifted

**White bean paste
(*shiro-an*)** 100 g

TOOLS

Pastry brush

Skewers

1. Preheat oven to 200°C. Line tray with parchment paper.

2. Prepare *matcha an* paste by combining matcha powder and white bean paste (*shiro-an*) in a bowl. Using a spatula, mix well to get an even bean paste. Divide into 6 portions and set aside.

3. Prepare *momoyama wagashi* dough:

    *   Spread white bean paste (*shiro-an*) evenly in a heatproof bowl. Cover with cling wrap and heat in a microwave oven at 500W for 1.5 minutes.

    *   Mix egg yolk and mirin and add one quarter of the mixture to white bean paste (*shiro-an*). Mix well. Heat in a microwave oven at 500W for another 1 minute.

    *   Add one quarter of egg mixture to white bean paste (*shiro-an*) and mix well. Reserve remaining egg mixture for use if necessary.

    *   Add cooked rice flour (*kanpai* powder) and knead into a dough. Divide into 6 equal portions, with 2 small amounts (1 g) for the ears and 0.5 g for the snouts, for each of the 6 portions.

4. Flatten each of the 6 portions of *wagashi* dough into a round disc and top with a ball of *matcha an* paste. Bring edges of dough up to enclose and seal filling. Roll to form a smooth ball.

5. Assemble and position ears and snout onto teddy *wagashi*. Using a skewer, poke holes for the eyes and snout. Repeat for the remaining *wagashi*.

6. Place teddy *wagashi* on tray. Brush with mirin. Bake for 13–15 minutes.

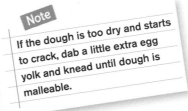

Note

If the dough is too dry and starts to crack, dab a little extra egg yolk and knead until dough is malleable.

Panda Bao

Makes 6 bao

Ingredients

Bao dough (page 14)

Charcoal powder 3 g

HOUJICHA FILLING

White bean paste
(*shiro-an*) 100 g

Houjicha powder 5 g, sifted

Candied chestnuts 4, diced
into 1-cm squares

TOOLS

Parchment paper

Edible food marker pens

Method

1. Prepare *houjicha* filling. In a bowl, add *shiro-an* and *houjicha* powder. Using a spatula, blend and mix well.

2. Add diced candied chestnuts. Mix well. Divide into 6 equal portions. Dab with paper towels if filling is too wet.

3. Prepare basic bao dough up to step 5 of that recipe (page 16).

4. Portion out 18 g of bao dough. Add charcoal powder. Knead well to colour dough evenly.

5. Shape both plain and charcoal dough into balls. Cover with cling wrap and allow to rest for about 30 minutes for fermentation to take place. The size of the dough should increase about 1.5 times. Punch dough down gently 3–4 times to remove air. Reshape both plain and charcoal dough.

6. On a lightly floured surface, portion plain dough into 6 balls.

7. Flatten a ball of plain dough slightly and top with a ball of *houjicha* filling. Bring edges of dough up to enclose and seal *houjicha* filling. Roll to form a smooth ball.

8. Place on parchment paper. Gently cover with cling wrap to prevent bao from drying while repeating the process for the remaining bao.

9. Shape black dough into ears of panda. Assemble onto white bao. Repeat for the rest of the bao.

10. Place bao in a large steamer and steam for 15–17 minutes.

11. Remove from steamer. Using edible food marker pens, draw eyes and nose to complete the panda character.

12. Serve warm.

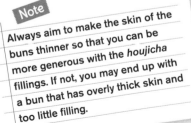

Note

Always aim to make the skin of the buns thinner so that you can be more generous with the *houjicha* fillings. If not, you may end up with a bun that has overly thick skin and too little filling.

Cat & Paw Bao

Makes 5 bao

~~~~~~~~~~~~~~~~~~~~~~~~~~~~~~ Ingredients ~~~~~~~~~~~~~~~~~~~~~~~~~~~~~~

Bao dough (page 14)

Cocoa powder 5 g

Charcoal powder 5 g

Vegetable oil as needed

TOOLS

Parchment paper

Edible food marker pens

1. Prepare basic bao dough up to step 5 of that recipe (page 16).

2. Portion out 40 g of dough. Add cocoa powder. Knead well to mix colour evenly. Portion out 10 g of dough. Add charcoal powder. Knead well to mix colour evenly.

3. Shape plain, cocoa and charcoal dough into balls. Cover with cling wrap and allow dough to rest for about 30 minutes for fermentation to take place. The size of the dough should increase about 1.5 times. Punch dough down gently 3–4 times to remove air. Reshape plain, cocoa and charcoal dough.

4. On a lightly floured surface, divide plain dough into 2 portions of 30 g balls and 2 portions of 20 g balls.

5. Flatten the both balls of 20 g plain dough into flat ovals. Brush with a little vegetable oil and fold each into half to form paws.

6. Portion out 10 g of cocoa dough. Flatten and shape it into 1 large circle and 3 smaller circles. Do the same for all the charcoal dough. Attach the circles to the folded plain dough to form 2 paw designs. Place bao on parchment paper. Gently cover with cling wrap to prevent bao from drying.

7. Pinch 2 smaller portions of about 1–1.5 g for the ears from each of the 30 g balls. Shape 2 cat's heads by rolling both balls, and attaching the ears.

8. Repeat the same process for the remaining 30 g of cocoa dough to form a brown cat's head.

9. Place the 2 paws and 3 cat's heads in a large steamer and steam for 15–17 minutes.

10. Remove from steamer.

11. Using edible food marker pens, draw eyes and nose and whiskers to complete the cat character.

12. Serve warm.

Chick Pull-apart Bao

Makes 6 bao

~~~~~ Ingredients ~~~~~

Bao dough (page 14)

Orange colouring a drop

Yellow colouring a few
 drops

TOOLS

Scraper

Parchment paper

Skewers

Edible food marker pens

Method

1. Prepare basic bao dough up to step 5 of that recipe (page 16).

2. Portion out 5 g dough and add orange colouring. Knead well to colour the dough evenly.

3. Portion the remaining dough into 2 equal parts. Add yellow colouring to one portion. Knead well to colour the dough evenly.

4. Shape into plain, orange and yellow balls. Cover with cling wrap and allow dough to rest for about 30 minutes for fermentation to take place. The size of the dough should increase about 1.5 times. Punch dough down gently 3–4 times to remove air. Reshape plain, orange and yellow dough.

5. On a lightly floured surface, portion plain dough into 3 balls, and yellow dough into 3 balls.

6. Position the dough slightly apart and in a circle on the parchment paper.

7. Divide and shape orange dough into 6 small balls. Using a scraper, create an indent to form the beak of the chick.

8. Assemble beaks onto yellow and white balls using a skewer.

9. Place bao in a large steamer and steam for 15–17 minutes.

10. Using edible food marker pens, draw eyes and feet to complete the chick character.

11. Serve warm.

Mushroom Bao

Makes 8 bao

~~~~~~~~~~~~~~~~~~~~~~ Ingredients ~~~~~~~~~~~~~~~~~~~~~~

Bao dough (page 14)

Cake flour 1 Tbsp

Water 1 Tbsp

Cocoa powder 2 tsp

Milk 1 $\frac{1}{2}$ Tbsp

TOOLS

Parchment paper

Scraper

1. Prepare basic bao dough up to step 8 of that recipe (page 16).

2. Portion out 30 g of dough and shape into 8 short tubes of 3–4 g each. These are for the stems of the mushrooms. Place on parchment paper.

3. Divide remaining dough into 8 portions, each 15 g. Flatten each portion into round discs to form the heads of the mushrooms. Brush with milk and dust with cocoa powder.

4. Place heads and stems in a large steamer and steam for 12 minutes.

5. Remove from steamer.

6. Whisk to combine cake flour with water. Dab flour mixture and attach each mushroom head to a stem.

7. Position bao apart on the parchment paper. Using a scraper, gently score the head of the mushroom bao.

8. Place bao in a large steamer and steam for another 2–3 minutes.

9. Serve warm.

Rose Bao

Makes 6 bao

~~~~~~~~~~~~~~~~ Ingredients ~~~~~~~~~~~~~~~~

Bao dough (page 14)

Matcha powder as needed

Purple sweet potato powder
1 tsp (or a few drops of pink
icing colour)

TOOLS

Scraper

Parchment paper

Toothpick

1. Prepare basic bao dough up to step 5 of that recipe (page 16).

2. Portion 8 g of plain dough. Add matcha powder. Knead well to colour the dough evenly.

3. Add purple sweet potato powder or pink icing colour to the remaining dough. Knead well to colour the dough evenly.

4. Shape into purple and green balls. Cover with cling wrap and allow dough to rest for about 30 minutes for fermentation to take place. The size of the dough should increase about 1.5 times. Punch dough down gently 3–4 times to remove air. Reshape green dough.

5. Reshape purple dough into 3 balls and divide each purple ball into 6 portions. Roll each portion into a thin, flat disc.

6. Place 6 discs in a row, with the sides of each disc slightly overlapping. Roll discs across to form a column. Repeat for the other 2 purple balls.

7. Using a scraper, gently cut each column into half. Place on parchment paper.

8. Shape green dough into leaves. Using a toothpick, gently press to make indents on the leaves. Assemble leaves with roses.

9. Steam buns in a large steamer for about 15–17 minutes over medium heat.

10. Serve warm.

Beer Jelly

Ingredients

Beer 500 ml, room
temperature

Gelatin powder 10 g

Note

For a non-alcoholic version,
you may replace beer with
apple juice.

~~~~~~~ Method ~~~~~~~

1. Place 100 ml beer in a heatproof bowl. Add gelatin powder. Mix well. Place mixture in the microwave oven and cook at 500W for 20–30 seconds until all the gelatin powder has dissolved.

2. Add remaining beer. Mix well.

3. Place in a bowl of iced water. Whisk quickly using a hand whisk to create foam. Keep whisking until there is a layer of foam about 1–2cm thick.

4. Pour jelly into serving mugs.

5. Gently top each mug with foam.

6. Cover and refrigerate for at least 2–3 hours to set. Serve chilled.

Quantities for this book are given in Metric and American (spoon and cup) measures. Standard spoon and cup measurements used are: 1 teaspoon = 5 ml, 1 tablespoon = 15 ml and 1 cup = 250 ml. All measures are level unless otherwise stated.

LIQUID AND VOLUME MEASURES

Metric	Imperial	American
5 ml	$1/6$ fl oz	1 teaspoon
10 ml	$1/3$ fl oz	1 dessertspoon
15 ml	$1/2$ fl oz	1 tablespoon
60 ml	2 fl oz	$1/4$ cup (4 tablespoons)
85 ml	$2 1/2$ fl oz	$1/3$ cup
90 ml	3 fl oz	$3/8$ cup (6 tablespoons)
125 ml	4 fl oz	$1/2$ cup
180 ml	6 fl oz	$3/4$ cup
250 ml	8 fl oz	1 cup
300 ml	10 fl oz ($1/2$ pint)	$1 1/4$ cups
375 ml	12 fl oz	$1 1/2$ cups
435 ml	14 fl oz	$1 3/4$ cups
500 ml	16 fl oz	2 cups
625 ml	20 fl oz (1 pint)	$2 1/2$ cups
750 ml	24 fl oz ($1 1/5$ pints)	3 cups
1 litre	32 fl oz ($1 3/5$ pints)	4 cups
1.25 litres	40 fl oz (2 pints)	5 cups
1.5 litres	48 fl oz ($2 2/5$ pints)	6 cups
2.5 litres	80 fl oz (4 pints)	10 cups

DRY MEASURES

Metric	Imperial
30 grams	1 ounce
45 grams	$1^1/_2$ ounces
55 grams	2 ounces
70 grams	$2^1/_2$ ounces
85 grams	3 ounces
100 grams	$3^1/_2$ ounces
110 grams	4 ounces
125 grams	$4^1/_2$ ounces
140 grams	5 ounces
280 grams	10 ounces
450 grams	16 ounces (1 pound)
500 grams	1 pound, $1^1/_2$ ounces
700 grams	$1^1/_2$ pounds
800 grams	$1^3/_4$ pounds
1 kilogram	2 pounds, 3 ounces
1.5 kilograms	3 pounds, $4^1/_2$ ounces
2 kilograms	4 pounds, 6 ounces

LENGTH

Metric	Imperial
0.5 cm	$^1/_4$ inch
1 cm	$^1/_2$ inch
1.5 cm	$^3/_4$ inch
2.5 cm	1 inch

ABBREVIATION

tsp	teaspoon
Tbsp	tablespoon
g	gram
kg	kilogram
ml	millilitre

OVEN TEMPERATURE

	°C	°F	Gas Regulo
Very slow	120	250	1
Slow	150	300	2
Moderately slow	160	325	3
Moderate	180	350	4
Moderately hot	190/200	370/400	5/6
Hot	210/220	410/440	6/7
Very hot	230	450	8
Super hot	250/290	475/550	9/10

The recipes in this book were taken from *Kawaii Sweet Treats,* first published in 2016.

Photographer: Calvin Tan

Published by Marshall Cavendish Cuisine
An imprint of Marshall Cavendish International

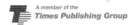

A member of the
Times Publishing Group

Other Marshall Cavendish Offices:
Marshall Cavendish Corporation. 99 White Plains Road, Tarrytown NY 10591-9001, USA • Marshall Cavendish International (Thailand) Co Ltd. 253 Asoke, 12th Flr, Sukhumvit 21 Road, Klongtoey Nua, Wattana, Bangkok 10110, Thailand • Marshall Cavendish (Malaysia) Sdn Bhd, Times Subang, Lot 46, Subang Hi-Tech Industrial Park, Batu Tiga, 40000 Shah Alam, Selangor Darul Ehsan, Malaysia

National Library Board, Singapore Cataloguing-in-Publication Data

Names: Wong, Shirley (Writer on bento cooking). | Tan, Calvin, photographer.
Title: Get started making fun treats / Little Miss Bento, Shirley Wong ; photographer Calvin Tan.
Other title(s): Get started making
Description: Singapore : Marshall Cavendish Cuisine, [2017]
Identifiers: OCN 1003327105 | 978-981-47-9415-2 (hardcover)
Subjects: LCSH: Desserts--Japan. | Cookies--Japan. | Cake--Japan. | Cooking, Japanese. | LCGFT: Cookbooks.
Classification: DDC 641.860952--dc23

Printed by Times Offset (M) Sdn Bhd